MILITARY JOBS

GREEN BERETS

▶▶ What It Takes to Join the Elite

ALEXANDER STILWELL

Cavendish
Square

New York

Published in 2015 by Cavendish Square Publishing, LLC
243 5th Avenue, Suite 136, New York, NY 10016

© 2015 Brown Bear Books Ltd

First edition

Website: cavendishsq.com

This publication represents the opinions and views of the author based on his or her personal experiences, knowledge, and research. The information in this book serves as a general guide only. The author and publisher have used their best efforts in preparing this book and disclaim liability rising directly or indirectly from the use and application of this book.

CPSIA compliance information: Batch #WW15CSQ.

All websites were available and accurate when this book was sent to press.

Library of Congress Cataloging-in-Publication Data

Stillwell, Alexander.
 Green Berets : what it takes to join the elite / Alexander Stillwell.
    pages cm. — (Military jobs)
 Includes index.
 ISBN 978-1-50260-161-2 (hardcover) ISBN 978-1-50260-231-2 (ebook)
 1. Special forces (Military science)—United States—Vocational guidance. I. Title.

 UA34.S64S75 2015
 356'.167—dc23

                    2014026353

For Brown Bear Books Ltd:
Editorial Director: Lindsey Lowe
Managing Editor: Tim Cooke
Children's Publisher: Anne O'Daly
Design Manager: Keith Davis
Designer: Lynne Lennon
Picture Manager: Sophie Mortimer

Picture Credits:
T=Top, C=Center, B=Bottom, L=Left, R=Right

Front Cover : FC All images Library of Congress
All images © Library of Congress, except; 10, © Bettmann/Corbis; 30, © Shutterstock.

Brown Bear Books has made every attempt to contact the copyright holder.
If you have any information please contact licensing@brownbearbooks.co.uk.

We believe the extracts included in this book to be material in the public domain.
Anyone having any further information should contact licensing@brownbearbooks.co.uk.

Manufactured in the United States of America

CONTENTS

INTRODUCTION

The U.S. Army Special Forces—unofficially known as the Green Berets—were created to carry out unconventional warfare, special reconnaissance, and direct-action missions.

The U.S. Army Special Forces are a specific unit among a number of special forces units in the U.S. military. They are trained for a wider range of missions than other U.S. special forces. They can respond to any situation. They learn unconventional warfare, which makes them ideal for confronting the terrorists and insurgents that often face U.S. forces in modern combat.

The Green Berets are organized into seven groups that each focus on different parts of the world. Each Special Forces Group is made up of four battalions, each of which has five companies of twelve "A-Teams."

The Green Berets are highly effective even in small numbers. They are trained to work with or recruit local fighters. That means a few A-Teams in a region can put together a sizable fighting force.

A member of the Green Berets looks for insurgents in the mountains of Afghanistan in 2011.

▶▶ HISTORY

The roots of the Green Berets lie in World War II (1939–1945). The U.S. Office of Strategic Services (OSS) trained small groups to work with local people in occupied areas. They used unconventional warfare, such as ambushes and raids.

▼ Wearing snow camouflage, a team of Green Berets patrol along the edge of a river during a winter warfare exercise.

During World War II, small teams were parachuted into France to support the French Resistance, while Operational Detachment 101 fought with the Burmese against the Japanese. American–Canadian special forces groups fought in Europe.

◀◀ With his face painted for camouflage, a member of the 5th Special Forces Group heads into the jungle on patrol during the Vietnam War (1963–1975).

After the war, U.S. military planners decided to pursue special operations. In 1952 the Special Operations Division of the Psychological Warfare Center was activated at Fort Bragg, and the 10th Special Forces Group (Airborne) was set up.

Fighting in Vietnam

In April 1960 the 5th Special Forces Group was created. As civil war broke out in Vietnam, it was sent to advise and train troops of South Vietnam, a U.S. ally, in the Army of the Republic of Vietnam (ARVN). When the United States joined the war, the group carried out unconventional warfare. It was one of the first units to start fighting and one of the last to leave at the end of the war.

IN ACTION

Since the end of the Vietnam War in 1973, Special Forces from various groups have deployed to El Salvador, Panama, Haiti, Somalia, Bosnia, Kosovo, Afghanistan, Iraq, and the Philippines. The 10th Special Forces Group was deployed to Northern Iraq to organize Kurdish forces in 2003.

WHAT IT TAKES

Getting to wear the Green Beret is not easy. Successful recruits are expected to be capable of performing a wider range of duties and to possess far higher skills than a regular soldier.

The fighting talent of a Green Beret matters more than his appearance.

Any male soldier can apply to join the Special Forces (there are currently no female Green Berets). But men need to be both smart and fit. They all have to be high-school graduates, and most have been to college. Written tests examine their aptitude for various tasks. Language skills are very important, as Green Berets are expected to be able to communicate with people anywhere in the world.

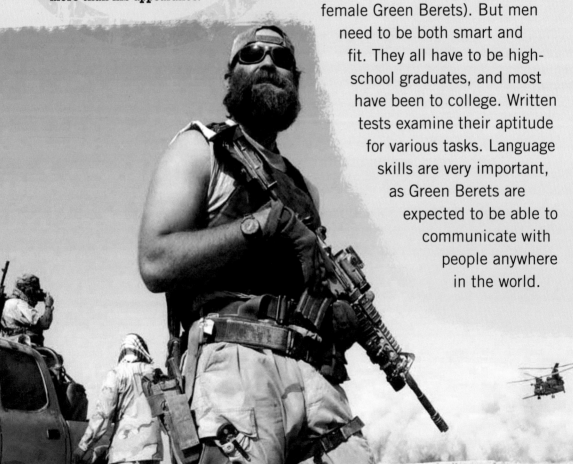

Desired Qualities

Fitness and intelligence are only two of the qualities a candidate for the Green Berets needs. The assessors at Fort Bragg also look for ten more qualities:

- motivation
- trustworthiness
- accountability
- maturity
- stability
- judgment
- decisiveness
- teamwork
- influence
- communication skills

 A member of the 19th Special Forces Group sets off on a navigation exercise after being dropped by a helicopter.

EYEWITNESS

"The journey to becoming a Special Forces soldier will not be easy. Special Forces training is rigorous and highly selective, but the courage and strength you will gain as a candidate will stay with you your entire life."

—U.S. Army Special Forces official brief

SPECIAL FORCES
ASSESSMENT
AND SELECTION

Qualifying for the Green Berets begins with the Special Forces Qualification Course, or "Q" Course. Candidates have to pass the Special Forces Assessment and Selection (SFAS) even to reach the main part of the course.

 Candidates for SFAS hold up a heavy log for as long as possible.

SFAS is designed to weed out weak candidates. Candidates are put through the mill for twenty-four days, but those who get through have a good chance of making it through the whole Q course. Candidates take a series of physical tests; if they fail any, they are out.

Navigation Exercises

The core of SFAS is fifteen days of exercises based on navigation. Candidates have to find their way across rough terrain by day and night, often in terrible weather. They have to carry heavy loads, and get very little sleep. This is how instructors can examine how they

 Candidates work in small groups to perform a series of tasks, including carrying logs.

react under physical and mental stress. Only soldiers with enough determination, courage, and stamina will get through.

EYEWITNESS

"Special Forces Assessment and Selection is geared to test your survival skills, and places an even stronger emphasis on intense physical and mental training."

—**U.S. Army Special Forces official brief**

▶▶ THE Q COURSE

Candidates who pass SFAS move on to the main part of the Q Course, which is officially called Special Forces Qualification Course (SFQC). They must also have completed Airborne School to learn how to parachute.

SFQC has five phases that together make up almost a year of continuous assessment.

The Phases

Phase I of SFQC is a seven-week introduction to special forces, their missions, and how they operate in the field.

During Phase II soldiers learn about small-unit tactics, including how to carry out patrols, raids, and ambushes. It also includes a demanding 18-mile (30-km) land navigation course through swamps and marshes.

Phase III focuses on the chosen specialty of each candidate, such as

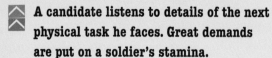

A candidate listens to details of the next physical task he faces. Great demands are put on a soldier's stamina.

engineering, weapons, or medicine. When the soldiers join an A-Team, they will be relied upon as the expert in their specialty.

Phase IV covers unconventional warfare. This includes tactics such

as guerrilla fighting and sabotage, but it also prepares soldiers mentally for the challenges of working with local forces.

Phase V is language school, a reminder that special forces need to communicate effectively with local people. Soldiers learn not only international languages such as Spanish or Arabic, but also more local languages, such as Pashto, the language of Afghanistan.

EYEWITNESS

"Becoming a Green Beret is an endless process of developing skills, testing them, employing them, and developing new skills."

—**Colonel Gerald Schumacher, Special Forces (Retired)**

 Members of the 19th Special Forces Group use global positioning systems (GPS) during a navigation exercise.

>> SERE
(SURVIVAL, EVASION, RESISTANCE, AND ESCAPE)

Special Forces operate behind enemy lines in groups that are too small to fight off an enemy force. That puts them at high risk of being captured. SERE helps them to avoid capture or to escape back to safety.

SERE training was created by the U.S. Air Force after the Korean War. The U.S. Army has its own version at Fort Bragg. The first part of the course trains Special Forces soldiers to find their way back to safety after missions behind enemy lines. They need to survive in hostile territory and evade the enemy. They may have a basic "escape kit," but they also need to learn how to survive with nothing. They learn how to find water, trap animals for food, identify which plants can be eaten, and how to

>> **Candidates learn to make a signal fire during Arctic training.**

make shelters. All these skills need to be adapted for different temperature zones. The challenges are different in an arctic, desert, or tropical environment.

Taken Captive

The second part of the course teaches Green Berets how to deal with capture and how to resist interrogation. The soldiers learn how to give away as little information as possible when

under interrogation. The best way is not to be interrogated in the first place, so the soldiers are trained to escape at the earliest opportunity. Escaping soon after being captured is often easier than when the enemy has managed to get a prisoner back to their base.

A soldier is captured during an exercise: the first moments are the best time to escape.

EYEWITNESS

"Green Berets work in environments that place them at high risk of being captured."
—Col. Gerald Schumacher

>> ONGOING TRAINING

Soldiers who pass SERE are full members of the U.S. Army Special Forces, but for a Green Beret, training and learning never stop.

 Soldiers in an airplane wear breathing apparatuses as they prepare to make a high-altitude parachute jump.

Some further training is based on geography. Soldiers do extra training for whatever region their Special Forces Group operates in, which might involve further desert or jungle survival training.

 A Special Forces team leave their vehicle on a training exercise in desert warfare.

Special Skills

Other training develops special skills, such as mountaineering. Soldiers can attend Sniper School to improve their marksmanship. There is always room to develop skills. In initial training they learn SCUBA diving, for example, but later they might complete the U.S. Army Combat Divers Qualification Course (CDQC). There they learn underwater infiltration techniques and advanced SCUBA diving.

EYEWITNESS

"As a soldier, one of the most important things you can do is make sure your soldiering skills are finely tuned."

—**U.S. Army Special Forces official brief**

17

WHO MAKES UP AN A-TEAM?

Most of the U.S. Army is divided into units, such as squads or platoons, that operate as part of larger groups, such as companies and battalions. The Special Forces are divided into Operational Detachments Alpha—or A-teams.

A communications specialist is in touch with the team's commanders at all times.

A-teams usually have twelve members. They are led by a commander, assistant commander, operations sergeant, and a noncommissioned officer. These leaders are responsible for the planning and execution of operations. They are supported by soldiers with special skills.

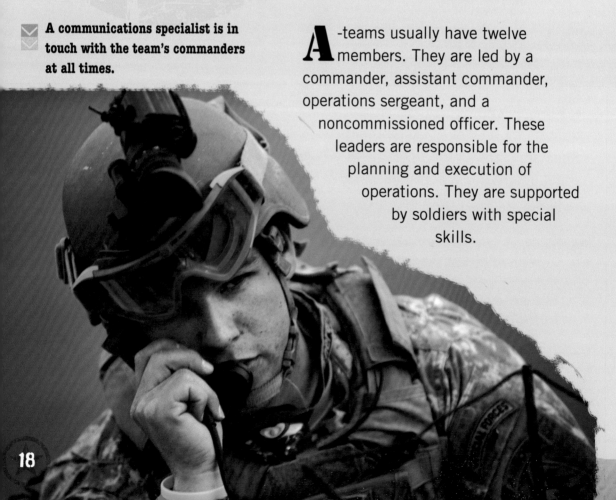

Part of an A-team takes part in a patrol through hostile territory in Iraq in 2010.

Specialist Roles

The tasks of each specialist are:

• Weapons specialist – an expert in both U.S. and foreign weapons, which special forces may need to use with local forces.

• Engineering specialist – an expert in demolitions work and in constructing field fortifications.

• Medical specialist – an expert in trauma care and other medical emergencies; he also carries a medical pack for the team.

• Communications specialist – an expert in all types of communications, who keeps the team in contact with base or with a Commando Solo aerial communications center overhead.

IN ACTION

A-teams tend to work in two groups of six. Each soldier in the two groups is trained in more than one special skill in case another member of the group is killed or wounded.

MARKSMANSHIP AND SNIPING

If you think that sniper school is just about hitting a target at long range, think again. The Special Operations Target Interdiction Course (SOTIC) at the Army Sniper School, Fort Benning, Georgia, is one of the toughest courses in the business.

A marksman lines up a target with his Mk12 Special Purpose rifle.

A Special Forces sniper needs a high level of self-control. He also needs to learn field and movement skills that will allow him to get into position unseen, and advanced camouflage so that he cannot be seen as he waits for a clear sight of the target, which might take days.

In Position

Peoples' lives depend on a sniper's ability to hit the target with his first shot. In a hostage situation, for example, a sniper needs to disable kidnappers or terrorists before they have time to harm the hostages.

Using a camouflage net for cover, a sniper and his spotter wait for a target to appear.

EYEWITNESS

"Becoming an Army sniper is about self-discipline, self-reliance, self-control. It is about tracking, stalking, deception, ranging, and surviving. It is about operating independently with patience and cunning. And finally, it is about shooting straight and shooting true—on the first shot every time."

—Army instructor

ADVANCED PARACHUTE JUMPING

All U.S. Army Special Forces learn basic parachuting at Airborne School. But they also need to be able to carry out a series of advanced techniques and handle sophisticated ram-air parachutes that operate in the same way as a glider.

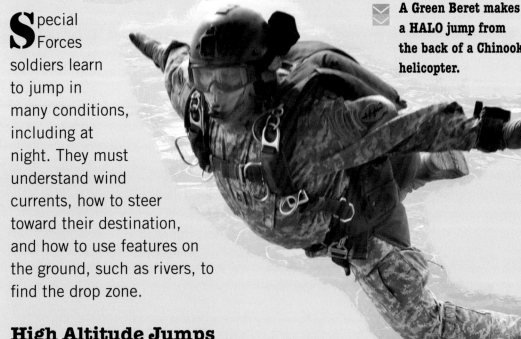

Special Forces soldiers learn to jump in many conditions, including at night. They must understand wind currents, how to steer toward their destination, and how to use features on the ground, such as rivers, to find the drop zone.

A Green Beret makes a HALO jump from the back of a Chinook helicopter.

High Altitude Jumps

Many jumps take place at high altitude, where aircraft cannot be spotted by enemy radar. The soldiers wear oxygen masks to breathe. HAHO jumps are High Altitude, High Opening; HALO is High Altitude, Low Opening. HALO jumps are carried out when the plane can pass over the target area. HAHO jumps are used where the aircraft is up to 30 miles (48 km) from the landing area, such as flying outside the border of a hostile country. The jumper pilots his ram-air parachute to the target. Low Altitude, Low Opening

 Special Forces make a HALO jump at dusk. Finding a drop zone safely at night requires a high level of skill.

IN ACTION

Special Forces may jump from a height of between 35,000 feet (11,000m) to 15,000 feet (4,600m). They wear a helmet and oxygen supply and breathe oxygen intensively before the jump to reduce the danger of breathing problems.

(LALO) is designed to minimize jumpers' exposure to fire from the ground. It is a risky technique. If something goes wrong, there is no time to deploy a reserve parachute.

DIRECT ACTION

A key role of the U.S. Army Special Forces is direct action (DA). The phrase covers a wide range of operations, from sabotage and ambush to hostage rescue. They are all intended to inflict damage on the enemy—and they are all potentially dangerous.

Green Berets clear a room on a Special Forces Advanced Urban Combat course.

Direct action missions might involve destroying a specific target, such as a communications or weapons base; capturing enemy equipment; or freeing hostages. In order to achieve maximum surprise, Special Forces approach the target by stealth. They may make a HALO jump into an area. Near the coast, they might parachute into the sea

The Special Forces use mock buildings to carry out training for operating in urban environments.

then use combat rubber raiding craft to come ashore.

Unwinnable Fights

An A-team is not large enough to take on enemy forces for long periods. The Green Berets aim to complete their mission and leave before the enemy can react. This is one reason the Special Forces are so demanding about the abilities of individual soldiers. The initiative and skills of soldiers are the best weapons against becoming trapped in an unwinnable fight against superior numbers.

EYEWITNESS

"Direct action missions are short-duration offensives designed to seize, capture, or destroy a target, or recover designated personnel or material."

—U.S. Army official brief

PSYCHOLOGICAL OPERATIONS

The Green Berets rely on making up for their small numbers by building alliances with local people. They often use psychological operations (PSYOPs).

Afghan children surround a Special Forces soldier during a PSYOPs visit to a village.

PSYOPs involves using information, propaganda, and diplomacy to get the support of local people for U.S. operations. Such alliance-building is sometimes referred to as winning "hearts

 A U.S. Army sergeant hands a radio to an Afghan to encourage communication with U.S. forces.

and minds." PSYOPs is an important part of many Special Forces operations.

Green Beret Psyops

Green Berets learn to communicate effectively, including by speaking local languages. They are taught to be sensitive to local cultures, so that they do not cause offense. They are encouraged to understand the needs of local people and to

work with them. This can involve providing practical help, such as building wells or providing medical care. Such operations aim to create an environment in which the enemy find it more difficult to win support.

IN ACTION

By nature, many Special Forces soldiers are quietly confident people. That makes it easy for them to mesh with people of other cultures. They can earn the trust and respect of others while retaining their own identity and professionalism.

UNCONVENTIONAL WARFARE

Unconventional warfare describes the way the Green Berets make alliances with local forces to fight a common enemy. It is one of their prime skills. It means they can have an effect on operations way out of proportion to their actual numbers.

Whereas direct action missions involve quick strikes, unconventional warfare can last months or even years as the Special Forces build loyalties. In a typical scenario, Special Forces are parachuted or dropped by helicopter into an area to make contact with key leaders among

 Green Berets began unconventional missions in the Vietnam War.

 An Afghan police sergeant holds discussions with members of the Green Berets.

rebel forces whose aims are similar to those of the United States and its allies.

Communication Skills

The Green Berets use their unique language skills and knowledge of the area and its customs to create good relationships with local fighters. They can provide their allies with logistical and technical support. These might include the deployment of close air support (CAS) for the local forces. In this way the Green Berets build a useful military alliance.

Working with Locals

It takes great skill to build trust and foster positive relationships in areas where loyalties may be fragile. The Special Forces are trained to overcome suspicion of foreign powers. They also learn to bring together rebel forces who may have fierce rivalries and who often argue among themselves.

IN ACTION

During Operation Enduring Freedom, U.S. Special Forces worked alongside opposition forces in Afghanistan to bring down the Taliban regime and rid the country of al-Qaeda fighters.

›› SPECIAL RECONNAISSANCE

A critical role of U.S. Army Special Forces is to enter enemy territory ahead of an attack by conventional forces. They must avoid detection at all costs.

If the Special Forces patrols are spotted, the enemy would realize an attack was coming and would have time to prepare its defenses. The Green Berets move into position using SERE (Survival, Evasion, Resistance, and Escape) techniques. They build hides to conceal their position. When they report to base, they use fast-burst transmission radio signals to lessen the chance that the signals will be intercepted.

Reporting Back

Once they are in position the soldiers use sophisticated electronic equipment to gather information about enemy forces,

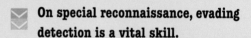
On special reconnaissance, evading detection is a vital skill.

including their size, location, the type of weaponry they possess, and the location of important communications centers. They also provide key information about the geography and terrain, including details such as whether an area can be used by heavy armored vehicles.

Once a battle starts, special reconnaissance teams who are already in position can carry out roles in identifying targets. They use radio to direct missile and air attacks on key targets.

EYEWITNESS

"Special Reconnaissance (SR) missions monitor as much as possible about the enemy's movement and operations, and are considered by many to be among the most important Special Forces operations."

—U.S. Army Special Forces official brief

 Green Berets set off to locate Iraqi missile positions on a special reconnaissance mission during the Persian Gulf War of 1991.

>> COUNTER-TERRORISM

Special Forces are involved in counterterrorism in different ways. This can take the form of direct action, in which they carry out hostage rescue or attack terrorist units, but it might also be part of a longer-term strategy.

Green Berets train in stopping and searching cars.

Direct action missions are short-term operations to achieve specific goals. This might include rescuing U.S. hostages or using an unmanned aerial vehicle, or drone, to attack a terrorist leader in a remote location.

 The fight against terrorism takes Special Forces into urban environments where terrorists can hide.

A Longer View
In the longer term, however, Special Forces use their expert knowledge to persuade local people not to support terrorists. They also train local forces to counter terrorist threats within their own countries.

EYEWITNESS

"Special Forces counterterrorism involves offensive measures to prevent, deter, pre-empt, and respond to terrorism. This includes covert missions in hostile, denied, or politically sensitive environments."

—Col. Gerald Schumacher

FOREIGN INTERNAL DEFENSE (FID)

Special Forces have been involved for many years in training forces around the world to deal with their own internal terrorists and drug-runners.

This program is known as Foreign Internal Defense (FID). One of its key aspects is counterinsurgency (COIN), where the Special Forces show government forces how to resist illegal activity. In Central and South America, for example, COIN operations focus on stopping drug trafficking. Special Forces train local forces in how to track and intercept narcotics traffickers. This training might involve techniques such as using boats to intercept smugglers on rivers.

 A Green Beret trains Lebanese soldiers in how to use a metal detector in mine-clearing training.

Containing Problems

The Special Forces train their local counterparts in skills such as direct action missions against insurgents, special reconnaissance, and counterterrorism. They also teach foreign forces to understand the psychology of insurgents to help to anticipate their actions.

The motivation behind FID is that it is better to contain problems on a local level before they can become larger and threaten U.S. global or economic interests.

EYEWITNESS

"*Special Forces soldiers have trained foreign governments to deal with drug warlords and traffickers as well as the growing threat of terrorist groups within their borders.*"

—**U.S. Army Special Forces official brief**

A member of the 10th Special Forces Group trains local troops in Mali, in northwest Africa.

▷▷ AIRCRAFT

In action, the U.S. Army special forces rely on aircraft. Airplanes and helicopters do not only get them wherever they need to be. A sophisticated airborne control center can also monitor and direct a whole mission on the ground.

The Special Forces "eye in the sky" is the EC-130J Command Solo. It is a modified large-bodied airplane filled with advanced communciations and imaging technology.

 Members of the 19th Special Forces Group use ropes to drop from a Pave Black Hawk helicopter.

 An AC-130H/U Spectre gunship fires flares as part of an exercise in 2007.

The aircraft carries a Battlefield and Control Center. This is like an airborne headquarters, with radios, radars, monitors, and other equipment. The personnel follow the mission on the ground and help ground-based commanders make key tactical decisions.

Spectre Gunship

The AC-130H/U Spectre is the same basic aircraft as the Command Solo, but it has been modified as a heavily armed gunship. It provides close-air support for special forces on the ground.

IN ACTION

The MH-60G Pave Hawk is the Special Forces' preferred helicopter when stealth is important. Advance communications and navigation equipment allows the helicopter to carry out low-level operations at night and still find a landing zone perfectly.

WHEELED VEHICLES

The Green Berets travel light, but they sometimes need vehicles to move around quickly and stealthily on the ground.

Green Berets use a Lightweight Tactical All-Terrain Vehicle (LTATV) as they patrol in Iraq. The vehicle is light but fast and highly maneuverable.

They have their own preferred all-terrain vehicles that are adaptable enough to cover rough terrain with no roads. The largest is the M-ATV Mine Resistant Ambush Protected Vehicle. It has an armored hull to protect its crew from

 The weapons mounted on top of the M-ATV can be fired remotely from inside the vehicle.

buried mines or hidden improvised explosive devices (IEDs). Weapons mounted on the roof of the vehicle can either be fired by a soldier in the turret or remotely from inside the cab. The vehicle can be adapted as a troop carrier, a command and control center, or for reconnaissance.

Two-Man Missions

The Lightweight Tactical All-Terrain Vehicle (LTATV) is a light, fast vehicle that carries two Special Forces soldiers. It has no armor and is lightly armed, but it is highly mobile in areas where larger vehicles cannot operate. Because it is so light, it can be carried easily in MH-47 and CV-22 aircraft, or parachuted into a mission area.

IN ACTION

The Special Forces' smallest vehicle is the all-terrain vehicle (ATV). It only carries one soldier, who drives it with motorcycle-style handlebars. The ATV handles well in rough terrain. It also enables Special Forces to move very quickly around a battlefield.

RIFLES AND HANDGUNS

A Green Beret is taught that his most important weapon is his brain. Once he is in a firefight, however, it is his rifle that can make the difference between life and death.

This soldier's M4 is fitted with an optical sight and a grenade launcher.

The Special Forces are trained to use a wide range of weapons. Weapons specialists are also familiar with foreign weapons that might be used by their allies or captured from the enemy.

M4A1 Carbine SOPMOD1

The M4A1 Carbine Special Operations Peculiar Modification is a gas-operated, magazine-fed rifle. It has all kinds of enhanced features for Special Forces' use. They include an

> **M4A1 CARBINE SPECIAL OPERATIONS PECULIAR MODIFICATION (SOPMOD1)**
> *Caliber:* 5.56mm NATO
> *Weight:* 6.36lbs
> *Length:* 33in stock extended
> *Effective range:* 500m

 A Green Beret takes aim with an M240 rifle mounted on the back of a vehicle for stability.

easily detachable M203 grenade launcher; a sound suppressor; and an AN/PEQ-2A laser/infrared designator that illuminates a target with a beam of light that cannot be seen by the naked eye, but is visible through a night-vision sight.

M24 Sniper Weapon System

The M24 is a veteran, bolt-action, six-shot repeating rifle. It is fitted with the Leupold Mark IV 10 power M3A scope, and it is also fitted with metallic iron sights.

M9 Pistol

This semi-automatic pistol is used for close-combat operations. It can be fitted with a Laser White Light Pointer (ILWLP) for pinpointing targets.

M24 SNIPER WEAPON SYSTEM
Caliber: 7.62mm NATO
Weight: 5.4kg
Length: 1,092mm
Effective range: 800m

M9 PISTOL
Caliber: 9x19mm Parabellum
Weight: 952g unloaded
Length: 217mm
Effective range: 50m

OVERTHROW OF THE TALIBAN

After the terrorist attacks by al-Qaeda in the United States in September 2001, the U.S. and its allies planned operations against al-Qaeda and the Taliban regime that harbored them in Afghanistan.

 Special Forces soldiers leave a helicopter on top of a mountain.

The 5th Special Forces Group was deployed at once. These Green Berets were to make contact with Afghan chiefs and coordinate their forces, who were often rivals, in a series of offensives.

Fighting the Taliban

The Green Berets landed at night in high mountains in the fierce Afghan winter. They soon linked up with local commanders of the so-called Northern Alliance. They helped the Afghans plan a series of offensives against Taliban forces. The Green Berets coordinated Allied air support as they pushed south. They played a key role in the liberation of six Afghan provinces by November and in the fall of the capital, Kabul, on November 13.

EYEWITNESS

"We needed Special Forces to be intrepid, to take risks, to feel that some rules didn't apply to them. The strength of a lot of guys was their willingness ... to live with much less protection."

—Senior U.S. commander, Afghanistan

A soldier watches for Taliban in the mountains of Afghanistan.

IRAQ

When U.S. forces invaded Iraq in 2003 to attack the regime of Saddam Hussein, the Special Forces were some of the first troops sent into Iraq. They worked with Kurdish fighters in the north of the country who wanted to bring down Saddam's government.

Three Special Forces soldiers talk to local men in a liberated Iraqi town in 2003.

Two weeks into the invasion, on April 6, 2003, twenty-six Green Berets, three Air Force bomb controllers, and Kurdish fighters were ordered to capture a crossroads

at Debecka Pass in northern Iraq. After many of the Kurds were killed or injured by friendly fire from a U.S. airplane, the Special Forces found themselves heavily outnumbered. They faced an Iraqi

 Special Forces watch a building burn during a mission to capture Saddam Hussein's sons.

motorized rifle company with four tanks and hundreds of men.

Under Fire

Two Green Berets used shoulder-firing Javelin missiles to force back the Iraqi attack after four hours. The Green Berets even advanced a short distance to cut a key highway. They remained under tank and artillery fire for another three days before reinforcements arrived. They dug up Iraqi land mines and used them to blast a route through Iraqi earthworks for supplies.

EYEWITNESS

"Two guys shut down the attack. Two guys turned an Iraqi organized attack into chaos. They halted an entire motorized infantry company."

—Major Curtis W. Hubbard, Third Special Forces Group

GLOSSARY

ambush A suprise attack by people who are lying in wait.

camouflage To use colors or materials to make something blend with the surroundings.

drone A remote-controlled, unmanned flying vehicle used for reconnaissance and for attacks.

fast rope To slide quickly down a rope.

fieldcraft The techniques needed to survive in the field, especially without being discovered by the enemy.

gunship A heavily armed aircraft.

hostage A person who is taken captive as a way of getting certain conditions fulfilled.

infiltrate To move into position for an operation without being spotted by the enemy.

infrared An invisible form of electromagnetic waves.

insurgent A person fighting against a government or an invading force.

logistical Relating to the supply of weapons and equipment.

mine A buried bomb that is detonated by pressure.

narcotics Illegal drugs.

navigation The act of finding out one's geographical location and planning a route.

reconnaissance To use observation to find out about an enemy's positions.

sniper A marksman who shoots at people from a hidden position.

spotter A person who accompanies a sniper in order to help him identify a target.

Taliban A member of an extremist Islamic group in Afghanistan or Pakistan.

target designator A laser or other beam of light used to guide a missile or bomb to its target.

trafficking Trading in illegal goods.

FURTHER INFORMATION

BOOKS

Besel, Jennifer M. *The Green Berets.* Elite Miltary Forces. North Mankato, MN: First Facts Books, 2011.

Delmar, Pete. *The U.S. Army Green Berets: The Missions.* American Special Ops. North Mankato, MN: Velocity, 2013.

Earl, C.F. *Green Berets.* Special Forces: Protecting, Building, Teaching, and Fighting. Broomall, PA: Mason Crest Publishers, 2010.

Gitlin, Martin. *Green Berets.* Great Warriors. Minneapolis, MN: Core Library, 2013.

Glaser, Jason. *Green Berets.* Warriors of History. North Mankato, MN: Edge Books, 2006.

Hamilton, John. *Green Berets.* United States Military Forces. Minneapolis, MN: Adbo and Daughters, 2011.

Nobleman, Marc Tyler. *Green Berets in Action.* Special Ops. New York, NY: Bearport Publishing Co, 2008.

WEBSITES

www.goarmy.com/special-forces.html
The official U.S. Army website pages on the Special Forces.

science.howstuffworks.com/green-beret.htm
Pages on the Green Berets from Howstuffworks.com.

www.military.com/military-fitness/army-special-operations/army-green-beret-training
Military.com details of the fitness requirements for Special Forces.

sfalx.com
A private site with articles on the history of the Special Forces.

Publisher's note to educators and parents: Our editors have carefully reviewed these websites to ensure that they are suitable for students. Many websites change frequently, however, and we cannot guarantee that a site's future contents will continue to meet our high standards of quality and educational value. Be advised that students should be closely supervised whenever they access the Internet.

INDEX